Garden Of Poems

By: Tiffany Joy

ISBN (print format): 978-1-7347705-2-0

ISBN (e-book format): 978-1-7347705-3-7

Cover by: Tiffany Joy

Poetry and writing by: Tiffany Joy

Dedicated to:

Those that need connection to another.

Table of Contents

Introduction

Poems are like flowers, beautiful and blooming in their own time. Just like a garden, life has its seasons where different poems grow and bloom. Events and experiences being the soil and rain that cause the poems to sprout and bloom. This book takes you through the garden of poems created in the soil of my life from 2013 to 2020.

These seven years saw changes and different seasons come and go. I moved from coast to coast and then around the area I know live. Life has morphed and matured, turning into something even more beautiful now. The changes and growth were not all pain free. Some poetry in this book reflects that. My pain pouring out is especially noticeable from August 2019 to the end of 2019. I had 3 deaths in my family in that August. I've said multiple times in poems and other writings I bleed with my ink. Writing is how I grieve and how I heal.

The rawness of the poems in this book is different from what I publish on my site. Most of the time those poems are happy, light, and inspirational. However, everyone has tragedies and struggles, so some poems in this book are darker and less hopeful than most on my site. These poems are ways to connect and for you to know you're not alone in your sorrow, which is why I'm sharing them in this book.

I pour out my heart while I write, so I hope you handle it with care, kindness, and understanding. Each poem reflects my heart and a flower picked for you, my reader. They are expressions of love and trust. Treat them well and please enjoy their beauty.

Extraordinary
(April 2013)

I look to the future

with my dreams pushed back.

What road do I travel;

Where does it lead?

Will my someday come to play?

Or will another story unravel?

Will my thoughts stay a thought

Will my life be normal?

Please, let the mediocrity subside

For I dream of being extraordinary

Let me be amazed with how far I travel.

Let this road lead me to a life worth dreaming of.

If nothing else I hope this road leads

to a dance with my mate

to a life lived

and ends with an extraordinary story to tell.

Bird or fish?

(April 2013)

Staring at the valleys

the mountains

the depths, the sea

I thought I could fly

but held my wings back.

If I jump will I take flight

soaring above my cares

flying away from my fears?

Or will I fall

into the dark deep sea

drowning in a new world

I do not know.

Will I become

a fish in the great unknown?

Am I a bird or a fish?

Can you tell me, please

or is it something for me to find out,

something for me to learn,

for me to decide?

Free

(June 2014)

Free your verse
to free your mind
to free your poem.
Yes, free yourself
to free your soul
to free everything
you ever have known.

Free your verse
to see
to breathe.
Free your poem
to learn
to grow.
Free your mind
to be who you are
to just simply be.
Free yourself now
to learn
to know.

Goes the Clock

(July 2014)

Tick tock goes the clock
as the waves rolls in
time may fly
or time may stop
the waves crashes on the shore either way.

Tick tock goes the clock
as the sun shines on
time may fly
or time may stop
the sun will heat the sand either way.

Tick tock goes the clock
it's far far away
time may fly
or time may stop
we won't pay attention either way.

A Beauty and A Beast

(June 2015)

I longed for a strong hero,
a beauty to lean on,
a beast to help me on my way,
so exploration was started.
Who could complete me?
Where was he?
Inner findings
led to inner peace
and I found my strong hero,
she was there
inside of me.

Yes, I find my beauty
the more I explore my beast.
Both inside, both me,
and I am complete.
I may not know how
to capture one's heart,
but I can capture their arms
and that's alright with me.
I know I always seem on guard,
unless you are in my guard,
then I am my hero,
and I remember
I already know my way
and I am the only version of me.

Yes, I find my beauty
the more I explore my beast.
Both inside, both me
and I am complete.

Pen Poem

(October 2015)

Pierce me with your
ink filled sword,
force your words to linger
as they twist inside,
because murder is never sweet,
unless it's in the mind
causing a new reality to live.
So murder my mind
with words of wonder.
Let the sharp bladed images
of your prose or verse
slice out the mundane,
so that I may live among your ink
until the new understandings take hold
and I am reborn with new light
into a new life.

Soul Freed

(Jan 2019)

I am more than meets the eye.
more than just a body
or just a mind.

My soul runs deep;
protected by the dark prison walls
built stone by stone from my past.
Each hurt a stone, piled high
each rejection the mortar
and sealed tight with fear.

Now I am seeing
I am more than meets the eye
as I tear down the walls
stone by stone
casting them aside,
finding my true mind.

My soul runs deep,

like a patient river

weakening the seal and mortar

til hurt by hurt they fall away

and I truly heal.

No longer tied tight to my past

no longer blinded by the wall.

Now I can run free

and see the true depths of all of me.

Now my soul is freed.

Introvert

(January 2019)

There is a reservoir of energy,

inside my body within my soul.

It is attached to a gear and gate.

Each happy hello,

every smiling statement,

turn the gears opening the gate.

A dip of energy

a drop of life

drips and drops pass the gate.

I'm happy to pour out my purpose,

joyful to share my energy,

my love, my life,

except when the gate is fully opened

except when the reservoir pours out pain instead

and the gears wind up tight

like a coil begging to explode.

In solitude I close the gate

when alone I release the tightened gears

except when I can't

when peace, quiet, and solitude runs to fantasy

when reality is a crowded theater

or just one more hello,

then my world ends

and I'm left crying on the floor

lost, but thankfully alone.

Sleep and thoughts will fill up the reservoir again

time and creativity will close the gate,

but only those tears will loosen the gears.

I watch and listen to the gate and gears

so that pouring out my purpose doesn't turn to pain.

At Me

(February 2019)

Tear filled eyes would stare back at me,

a soul broken by all I've said,

if the words were spoken

instead of just in my head.

I'll rip down the confidence

that took so long to build

for I'm too impatient to wait

on an enemy to do it instead.

I can destroy my heart better anyways

I can whisper weapons

into my wounds

even before I leave my bed.

Or I could quiet the bully

sush the judge

overcome the victim

with the kindness I show my friends.

I can learn to love myself again

clean up the split confidence

sweep up the pity

and see my own beauty;

learn about my own knowledge

then joy filled eyes

would stare back at me instead.

Relax with Who You Are
(February 2019)

Let the sun shine on your face

feel my warm embrace

as I smile and say

You can breathe.

Trust me life is not a race.

Be relaxed with who you are.

There's no need to set high the bar.

You have your dreams.

You hold them too tight.

Yet true happiness and joy is not that far

So let the sun shine on your face

and be relaxed with who you are.

Melancholy
(February 2019)

Sadness, despair, and with a melancholy air

should not describe the girl with bouncy hair.

How I wish this dark grumpy cloud would disappear

so she would not be surrounded by wintry cold air

Darkness and death loom taking away that which she cares.

Oh bring back the sunshine

the love, happiness, and the warm hugging air.

Wash away the broken tears

with jokes and joyful jeers.

Turn the light of gratitude back on

and refocus the lens of reality on the good.

Let her love loom,

no more sadness, or despair

no more melancholy air.

No More Rungs

(February 2019)

There are no more rungs on my ladder
no more that I can see.
I can look down at the flowers
of past success
look up to where I want to be.
The only thing I can grab are vines
that'll make me fall and break.
If you were besides me
perhaps you could hand me a few rungs
but I'm here all alone.
Snug in my new home
on top of this ladder
with no more rungs to be owned.
Yes I made a mistake,
thought I had enough
thought to the top I would make
but here I am
with no more rungs to be owned.

Not Lost

(March 2019)

I am not lost
yet I journey on.
My path leads into the depths
into my own forest.
I am a tree rooted in family
but growing towards the sky,
a bird who has freedom to fly
but returns to her nest.

I walk on
learning more of me
seeing each side of me.
I am a diamond with a multitude of facets,
A puzzle I'm painting and piecing together.
I am not lost
yet I journey on.

Hold On

(May 2019)

I'm barely holding on.
I'm slipping, sliding away,
so hold on to me.

I'm weak, nearly missing,
still feel myself slipping,
so hold on to me.

Keep me tight in your arms
because I cannot hold on.
I'm stumbling, falling,
so hold on to me

Lord, please hold on to me.

Hope Ran Away

(May 2019)

When my world crashes down
darkness surrounds.
Reality is a cruel nightmare
and I cannot find my way out.
I'm in a forest of despair
huddled in the shadows of fear.
Hope ran away
and I am alone.

That is when you reach down,
clear away the despair,
lead me out of my fear,
and return hope to me.
You are the creator of the world
yet you care for me
when reality crashes down.

Try To Care
(July 2019)

I want to know
should I try to love you
or somehow let you go?
I thought I've forgiven all the tears
from the hurts I've locked inside for years
and maybe I have.
Perhaps they're truly are no more tears to cry
but I want to care or at least try
to be close enough for those tears.

Yet we're miles away
and worlds apart,
so you don't suck me down
to your low opinion of life,
but how do you walk away
from one who gave me half my DNA?

Let You
(July 2019)

Let the rivers and roads
lead you home.
Let the ocean breeze
call you close to me.

I've lassoed the moon
and it waits for you.
Let your calling dreams
guide you near to me.

We'll live together
in a sweet melody.
As long as you let
the rivers and roads
lead you home to me.

Purple

(August 2019)

Can I dream

in purple memories;

stay among the flowers and lightning?

Can I breathe in

the warm vacation air;

escape from reality?

No, the storm outside will haunt

it'll stay like a wound

until it heals the loss

and I'm left with the scars of purple memories.

Look For Me

(August 2019)

Do not look for me

in the ashes of who I once was.

I am not there.

I'm in the memories you hold dear

and the jokes we once shared.

I'm in the love you have,

the breeze that moves among the trees,

and in the warm loving air.

Do not look for me

in the ashes of who I once was.

I am not there.

Let Her Be

(August 2019)

Death you can not have her.

Let her be

she is not yours.

Misery stay away from her.

Let her be

she does not belong to thee.

Life embrace her.

Let her be

wrap her in your arms.

Happiness and joy touch her heart.

Let her be

she deserves your company.

Love embrace her and stay close.

Let her be.

Love and life be with her

she is yours and belongs to thee.

Depart Oh Darkness

(August 2019)

Depart oh darkness
you are not welcomed here.
Storm I will not surrender to thee.
You can leave me be.
I am not yours
and never will be.

I am not a flower.
I am a strong tree.
Though you may try
I will not bend, break, or die
I am here to stay.

So depart oh darkness
you are not welcomed here.
Storm I will not surrender to thee.
You can leave me be.
I am not yours
and never will be.

Without You

(August 2019)

A tiger can be caged.

A bird can live without flight.

I can live without you.

Plants can bloom inside.

Fish can thrive contained.

I can live without you.

He can hold his breath.

She can closes her eyes.

I can live without you.

Life will go on.

I will see the sunshine and storms.

I can live without you.

Yet, something inside longs to thrive.

Something inside longs to be free

and can only be when I live with you.

Pain About Waiting

(September 2019)

I ask how many days

does my heart have to break?

How much pain will go unhealed

until I surrender all?

What else can I lay at your feet?

How am I still holding on

and why does it tear my heart apart?

Questions like wounds appear and cut deep.

Reality crushes expectations

and I am left wondering.

I take on the burden of defeat.

Why do I try when nothing will be right?

Is this just a painful waiting game?

Is the only release death

or am I holding on to what is wrong?

Would my wounds heal,

pain be released,

if I laid what I don't want at your feet?

Could I give you my life

and all my control?

Would there then be relief?

There is pain in the waiting

and healing in surrender.

Garden Of Growth
(October 2019)

There's blood on my hands
but that's okay.

There's trauma in the pain
but I'm okay.

The walls are crashing down
but the house is standing its ground.
Darkness and death is all around
but that's okay.

There is beauty in the darkness
when the light shines thorough;
a master piece among the brokenness
when the good memories out last the tears.

Call the trauma a garden of growth
and see the flowers of change.

29

Rebuild the wall stronger.

It's okay.

The blood on my hands

is mine alone

from stitching up the wounds held inside.

I'll let the bloody pain

water my garden of growth.

Battle Inside
(November 2019)

I'm in a battle

with the person living inside of me

twisted up in the past

worried and wondering.

How do I survive?

There is a deep dark war

taking place behind my smiling eyes.

Death maybe coming

but it's unclear to which side.

Do I show you my plans for death that I hide,

the pain I'm always pushing aside?

If I look at the darkness too long

it will consume all of me.

Do I simply smile

hiding the pain and darkness inside?

Do I give into my soul's death?

Pretend my heart does not ache to create?

31

Living a life I'm not directed to live?

Or do I explode my passion

and shine all over the place?

It is a battle that rages inside of me.

It is deep.

It is dark.

The battle is for all of me.

Death maybe coming

but it's unclear to which side.

The Road

(November 2019)

The road is long.
The path is hard
and I keep thinking
I haven't gone that far.

Maybe I'm good
but need to be great.
Perhaps I'm struggling in vain
and being an artist is not my fate.

I could run.
I could hide
but then there would be
a deadly gnawing inside.

I'll stay my course
and walk my path.
Perhaps one day I'll look back,
see my struggles, and laugh.

Not The One

(January 2020)

I was not the one who grew up in a home of fear

well not completely

still I was weakened.

I was not the one torn from home;

the one with painful self inflicted releases

but still I cracked.

I was not the one struggling through withdrawals,

the one that watched her hearts be taken away

but still I broke.

I was not the one on the floor,

the one without breath

but still I crumbled.

In silence I was weakened

Without a word I cracked

With quiet tears I broke.

And with sobs I crumbled.

The Fight

(February 2020)

Fantastic fantasies form

happy and bright

but always involves a fight

with my heart and with my mind.

Perfection cannot last,

tragedy must strike,

especially when everything is bright.

Deep down I must believe

there's either trauma

or the silence before the storm.

If a garden grows, locust will come.

If I climb a mountain, I'll drown in a stream.

If I succeed in a career, no love will be near.

Yet, I still grow my garden

and climb my mountains,

because storms will come

whether I'm working or waiting.

Why Are We Friends?

(March 2020)

Why are we friends?

It's a question asked over and over again.

Asked by me, asked by you.

Then asked all over again by those we love.

I typically chuckle

as I say it's because you wouldn't let it end

but there's more and always has been.

Some easily see my sunshine.

People easily perceive your poison.

You put the armor of anger on

while I simply run and hide.

When you push away

I pull closer.

So why are we friends?

Because it's fun to shine into the darkness

and the monsters of my mind are murdered by your poison.

When your armor falls away

a beautiful creature is revealed

and I know your listening ear is safe.

So why are we friends?

Because bitch I won't let this friendship end.

Shy

(April 2020)

I don't want to be shy
I don't want to hide.
I yearn to explode each side of me,
show you all there is to see,
like a flower or a tree
growing only to give you shade;
like a tomato plant
creating my fruit for you.

I want to help you
give you all I am.
Perhaps then
one will be healed
or two could be.
Yet, I don't say anything,
nothing at all,
instead I decide to hide
and continue to be shy.

Boxed In
(May 2020)

I box myself in
like a wrapped present
hidden from its reason
Futile until made known.

Oh what joy I could give.
What love I could spread,
but when fear seeps in
I'm hidden instead.

Locked Away

(May 2020)

I was locked away

before I was told.

About to venture out

with plans to expand myself.

Now those plans are covered in dust

as they sit on a lonesome shelf.

I want to reach out to touch a new song,

to live a life outside my fantasies.

Now I'm locked away

because I was told to.

Will my connection always be

just a lonely plan

on a dusty, forgotten shelf

or will a key turn?

Will there be a release,

a time when my plans

can climb off the shelf

and allowed to be?

Childish

(May 2020)

Laughter seems childish
when the weight of adulthood bears down,
when sadness and misery can be seen all around.

How do I go back?
Can I find my way to that long known place,
where I can find my child like faith,
where God is closer than the world's fears?
Can you tell me if it's far or near?
The only thing I hear
is the world chasing its terrible fears.
It hides away the laughter.
Its pressure hides the cheer
so I want to go back
to my childish laughter
and be a child of faith.

Behind My Smiling Eyes
(May 2020)

Look at me
I'm happy and cheerful.
I'll love you as long as I can.
I'll help you and place you above me.
And you'll see my love
behind my smiling eyes.

Yes, look at me
You'll see I'm happy and joyful
because that's what I'm taught to be.
That's what I want to be.
Please focus on my smiling eyes.

I do still cry.
Apathy hugs me close
when I am in my room alone.
Fear that you'll turn away
is almost always near.
But I'll hide the fear

42

behind my smiling eyes.

See me when I'm truly happy
and know sadness still lays
behind my smiling eyes.

Where Are You?

(June 2020)

God, where are You

when the world seems dark?

Lord, where are You

when I've lost my way?

Savior, where are You

when I feel alone?

My King, where are You

when your throne seems far away?

Father Above, where are You

when my heart breaks and turns numb?

Father above, My King, Savior, Lord, and God

where are You in this day?

God, You are the light of a new day.

Lord, You are the lamp that lights my way.

Savior, You are the one holding me up.

My King, You are by my side.

Father Above, You are hugging me tight.

Father Above, My King, Savior, Lord, and God

You are with me making day from my night.

Peace

(October 2020)

Pleasing stillness

wraps and cleans my mind.

It centers my heart.

I am fully aligned.

Peace, a gift from God,

enters my body

relaxing my soul.

I pray, let peace be with you.

Let it be with you

as it is with me;

a heavenly gift from a loving father.

Learn

(October 2020)

Learn to recharge

not resign.

Learn to heal

not hurt.

Learn to stand your ground

not stumble around.

Learn to learn and live

not hide and die.

Importance Of You
(October 2020)

Oh the importance of you.

Oh the love and comfort I feel.

A partner without partnership;

a love without a love.

Two who could be, but never will

all because the importance of you.

To stumble would mean a fall

with one wrong step I would unravel,

I would come undone,

so silent will I stay

hopefully waiting for one day,

continuing being here for you,

as you continue to be what I need,

a love without a love

a partner without partnership,

all because the importance of you.

What I know

(December 2020)

What do you do

when failing, but failure is not an option?

What do you do

when the path is dark and you think you've fallen?

What do you do

when you don't know what to do or your options?

Those are the questions

but I have no answer.

I am lost

in the blurry darkness

waiting for guidance,

waiting for light.

Nothing I do seems correct.

Nothing I do appears right.

Still I do what I can.

I do know

the answers will come,

one day they will be here.

I do know

the light will shine,

like a rainbow after the storm.

I do know

all will end well,

as it always has.

What I say

(December 2020)

My breath tells me I'm still alive.

My heart says I will thrive,

but my brain is shouting I must strive.

The harsh reality of the world causes fear

and although my soul says God is near

my logic and mind drowns out the truth.

He has never left me alone,

but others have.

He has always provided for me,

but now I cannot see how.

Still my soul says God is near.

My heart tells me I will thrive.

My breath whispers that I am alive,

so I will trust that everything will be alright.

About The Author

You can thank my mom for my creativity. She enrolled me in dance when I was 5 and it seems like my creativity snowballed from there. I started musical theater when I was 10 and wrote endless narratives around that time too. Sometime during high school, I picked up writing poetry. In 2009 I graduated college with a Theater and Dance degree with a concentration in acting and directing but always wrote in my free time. Writing and art have always been my first passion, and in 2018 I left my salary job. I am now pursuing my passions as an author and artist.

If you would like to stay up to date with all that I do please find me on Instagram or Twitter @TiffyJoyBerry or check out my website ForTheJoyOfTiff.com.

www.ingramcontent.com/pod-product-compliance
Lightning Source LLC
Chambersburg PA
CBHW060539030426
42337CB00021B/4348